HUMFREY CONINGSBY

Jonathan Davidson was born in 1964 in Didcot, South Oxfordshire, and now lives in Coventry. He won an Eric Gregory award in 1990, and is the author of two previous collections of poetry and two pamphlets.

He is the author of eight radio plays broadcast on BBC Radio 3 and 4, along with adaptations of Geoffrey Hill's *Mercian Hymns* and W.S. Graham's *The Nightfishing* for radio. Find him on Twitter @JFDavidson1964.

Humfrey Coningsby

JONATHAN DAVIDSON

Valley Press

First published in 2015 by Valley Press
Woodend, The Crescent, Scarborough, YO11 2PW
www.valleypressuk.com

First edition, first printing (March 2015)

ISBN 978-1-908853-48-6
Cat. no. VP0060

A CIP record for this book is available from the British Library.

Printed and bound in the EU by Pulsio, Paris.

www.valleypressuk.com/authors/jonathandavidson

Contents

Acknowledgements

I am grateful to Duncan Law for directing me to a small church in Shropshire and so introducing me to Humfrey Coningsby (1567 – 1610?). Duncan also undertook research into Coningsby's life, revealing much, not least that Coningsby was in no mood to be discovered. I am also grateful to Tim Dee, Maura Dooley, Peter Sansom, Ruth Brandt, Roz Goddard, and other friends and family for their support.

A Neighbour's Description

Coningsby: landowner, of the squirearchy,
west Middle English accent, a few Welsh words.
We always took him for a strange one.
We knew he wouldn't die in his own bed,
but not either in anyone else's.
Did we ever see him with a maid? Yet,
he came back one time with the amble
of a man who'd swived and been swived
and with some words for it we didn't know.
I wasn't his friend. No one was. Once,
I lent him a small horse to take him
to the other side of the valley to see
a man about a dog. He was gone four years;
came back on foot without a word.
Still, we honoured him, you had to.

Why Coningsby Left England in the First Place

To find quaint fowl and other beasts and kill them;
to taste the salt of Latin, Hebrew, Greek on my English
    tongue;
to walk in the footsteps of our Lord's great Joy and Sorrow;
serpents and sea-dragons, the umber-coated goats of plenty;
meek women, strong men, poor simple shepherds piping
    songs;
kingdoms like fields of un-discovered barley;
to thresh and winnow out of time, a story.

Dear Village of Neen Sollars

I hold you in my arms and love you,
my hands upon the flanks of all your hills,
and through your streams I slip
my lately trimmed and polished fingernails;
and round your body all my body bring.

But we must part, this first last time;
you go to your straw-stuffed bed
to sleep the sleep of cut stone
and I will be transported
slowly these aching miles.

A Car is Hired

I had the boy drive.
A lonely road in Bohemia –

after the third fatality,
this one luckily only
a peasant woman,
I said to him simply:
my turn, and prised
his fingers from the wheel.
*Can I open my eyes now,
Sir,* he squeaked, half joking.

It was not as easy as it looked.
Bohemian roads are forever
running off into the forest
chasing wild boar and sprites.

We caught a few, sprites that is,
and it was their chirping
that put me off my guard.

The tree bowed courteously enough
and then hit me square
between the eyes.

Woke up later,
all quiet.

Waiting for a Sign

Not since I left England have I been able
to get decent *Wi-Fi* or *Bluetooth*.
I consult timetables and alchemists,
I question servants and the gods,
they give me philosophy and superstition.
They believe I may be man-handled
across this foaming stream,
or I may not; it is in the hands
of *who knows who*, they say, with a shrug
like soil sliding down a hillside.

Meanwhile, my tablet has packed up.
likewise my laptop. Christ Almighty!
I almost long for home,
the frozen hills of Shropshire,
but know it is no better there.
Here, at least, I understand
why I am not understood.

Coningsby's Future

Grey morning yawns at the open door.
A display of geese in the air,
and in the cottage-orchards
the June drop patters to the ground.

Last year's leather-coats simmer
in a pot above a fire; a little water,
some eastern spice brought back
from his last sojourn, their
sweet apple-ness discovered.

Why must he go on these travels
and return with talk of fighting
and women speaking in tongues,
or just tongues?

          I tell him, save
such stuff for your last days
when you have sired a family
of whelps and pups and are only
a cracked and brittle husk. But
off he goes again: Cyprus, Athos,
Troy and Syria. These are not places
but stories, and poor ones at that.

At Aleppo

Locked in the intestinal streets of Aleppo,
I appraise beauty in a puddle of gasoline
and an abandoned sandal.

Here I am alive, my Lords,
with your devices and decisions,
the creaking of rudimentary armour.

I had been prepared for this
by war and displaced peasants
encountered at every longitude.

However, I am perturbed
by a darkness that is bright sunlight
and a silence composed only of cries.

Souvenir of Troy

And see the snow fall
on the towers of Troy
when the globe is shaken.

Weeks of saddle-sores
and punctures and many-
headed dogs and lice.

This was not how I
imagined it. The girls
do not even look at me.

Is it because I stink
like a latrine? I'm buying
one postcard. That's it.

Darkness and Bells

Darkness and bells. Nothing to eat
but pistachios and stuffed sultanas.

In the distance, lights illuminate
twisting bodies and notices

proclaiming the goodness of Gods –
various – and prophets – particular –

including door times and rates
on the gate. I laugh out loud

at the absurdity of hope,
knowing so many will be dead

before tea-time. We have been told
history will not record the names

of those who leave their soft souls
unsanctified through cowardice, which

to be honest puts the dampener
on my enthusiasm for slaughter.

In Arcadia

Amongst primitive shepherds and their polyphonic songs
I disport myself. How often have I lain awake,
slightly scorched by flickering fire, to hear
their tales of herding ... and herding?
It reminds me of home; their stoic
acceptance of a brutal lot,
casual fornication, an abhorrence
of anything resembling sanitation.
Nowhere does it say in the guide books
how to thank a man for giving you his life,
and nowhere does it explain how to introduce
civilisation other than with the simplicity of violence.

Siege of Strigonium

This is more like it. I've seen men
burning like torches, oiled like
fresh kebabs, dancing into the river.
And if they are still living or not,
we pull their arms off and push
their eyeballs into their skulls. This
is warfare. By all that is holy
I bequeath these methods and choice
sophistications to our soon-
to-be-born and later politicians,
our military minds. A simple
maxim: maximum pain, maximum
pleasure. Don't let the screaming
put you off your suppers, my Lords.

Talks about Talks

Cantering suddenly through the language groups –
unable, obviously, to understand a word of Hungarian –
I bring the warring factions to a parley.

They lay down what they call their Kalashnikovs
and mortar bombs. I deposit on the same table
a kerchief of finest cambric or batiste.

And so we fall to talking and it transpires
that all man's misery is but fear and cant,
that we very much delight in fear and cant.

Go to it, then, I say, retrieving from
the table my kerchief and discharging
my nose into its sweet smelling folds.

And they do.

Meeting the Sultan's Daughter

Laying her hand on my burning forehead
and finding there the fires of Lucifer
and fearing for my life, she chose not
the surgeon's succulent leeches or his cups
but began straightaway to untie the bows
and ribbons of my tunic and had her girl
pull off my boots and hose, and tore my
undershirt, wet with my sad suffering,
and laid me out as naked as a cherub
and quickly washed me, knuckle and soft muscle,
as if the fever needed cleanliness
to kill it; which it did. And when I was
un-fevered, un-sweated, and un-muddied,
undressed and cleaned, did she in her
own sad Eden lie on me like a coverlet
or shroud and make fun with my mortality.

Coningsby in Love

He lifts his face from the lap of Mahomet's daughter
and thinks of buttercups and winterbournes
and the tight-hedged lanes of his native country
and cattle grazing on short, wet grass.

Her inarticulate cries were the voices
of the common birds of England; a crow,
a jackdaw, a second jackdaw, a flock of geese
high in the Salopian sky, in flight to heaven.

Later, she reads him a treatise on astrology,
how the earth curves and the moon moves.
He answers, endearingly, in squawks and whoops;
his tongue is not her own but she knows it.

Then, she prays for the symmetry of desire
as he dances and his feet describe her
in patterns, his arms like little wings,
his feathers lifting in the desert air.

Fly Business Class

They would not take my horse
or my boy; something about legroom
and passports. My sword they
unburdened me of and my boots
too. In fact, I found myself
bound hand and foot and
being shaken in a chamber.
This is not flight! We will
never make Burgundy or Rheims
or the Channel Ports, like this.

Corley Rocks: *No Fly Tipping by Order*

On my way home through Warwickshire,
the B17 giving sterling service,
but still sore. Pulled up
beneath the rocks. Leant the bike
against the sign. Comprehended
not a word of it and I speak six languages –
including one known only to myself
and the Sultan's daughter – no matter.
Walked the short way to the rocks.
Sat beneath them for their shade
as it was near noon; is that right?
Must have nodded off. Dreamed of war
and war's friend, disease;
how lucky I had been. Woke up.
re-traced steps. Bike gone.
Damnation.

Coningsby Returns to England, the Last Time

And when he had risen up the last hill
and could see clearly his parish, all
its teeth and bones, from his horse's
back he slipped and would not walk
but stood statue. His skin still showed
the colour of his travels. He wore strange
whiskers and had marks on his arms
from warfare. His horse would go on
so he let it go on, and he was left
looking through his years of life
at the heart and arteries of England
which pulsed slowly. *Something is
wrong about this country, it is
too green. Where are the camels
and the shaggy goats? Where is
the native wisdom? All I see here
are cheery bumpkins and wild hops.
That's not enough. I want sherbet.*

Coningsby at Sea

Coningsby walks by the inconsistent sea.
He hears the amber on the shingle beach
as it rubs itself against the other stones.

Whatever a sixteenth-century gentleman would wear,
that is what Coningsby is wearing beneath his doublet
and hose. And then he is naked.

He takes off his greatcoat with the popped collar
and his slip-ons from another age. His horse
has left him for a new owner and he is alone.

A barque from Bruges or Ghent encounters him
half-way to exhaustion and he is dragged aboard.
What are you doing, man? They say, in Flemish.

I am honouring the flotsam-spitting sea
and tipping my cap at a watery grave
and also finishing off a man's life.

The Hellespont

Only a bloody fool would swim the Hellespont
when for a coin you can have a boat
row you over. When you are journeying,
as I have been these – on and off –
fifteen years, you don't waste time
on actions that are glorious
but likely to kill you. I said the same
to Rudolf at the Siege of Strigonium,
or would have done if he'd spoken
Latin, Hebrew, Greek or Welsh,
but he didn't. He was another one.

War/Apricots

I.

A cold March day, what few blooms
battered by an Anatolian easterly.
Our flags lurched and stooped,
our horses stamped their feet,
bellows-snorting. On all quarters
hoards, their speech whinnying
dark psalms across the plain.

II.

I do not think, today, of war,
but of a woman who once placed
a slim hand on my forehead
and released me from myself.
That was a day; the apricots
in the copper bowl could not
have tasted sweeter than her
soft touch, too briefly known.

Coningsby: Missing

Into the air, a fluster of finches,
unlikely to see another summer.

The missing are all about us;
cairns of charred bones, texts,
signatures on applications for leave
to remain. He may have been deported
or turned away at a checkpoint – an
oddity in his doublet and hose, his
ruff now sad plumage, and his boots
stained with tears. He is sat with others
dispossessed of hearth, exchanging not
cheering stories of clustered orchards
but curses and recriminations, oaths.

Out of the air, a phalanx of helicopters,
lights picking out the sleeping souls.

The Last Dream

Where had I got to? That boy has gone again.
I believe I have asked for sweet mint tea
and perhaps some of those little... things.
The aroma of her perspiration soothed me,
collapsed my seasons into scattered straw
and flew me all about the ridge and furrow,
and headland. I go back to my childhood
but cannot claim it. That too is lost to me.
The desert shifts its shoulders like a sea.
I think of my Captain from Bruges or Ghent;
no more of him. *Her* voice was secretive,
drew music from my bones. I will see her
again. Here or there. Now and again. Now,
this sleep envelops me. Sweet mint. Tea.

We Have No Record

So many have disappeared: drowned,
starved, killed or carried off.
We estimate numbers, appeal for
sightings, map and track, tag
and locate, but still they fall
off the edge of the known world.

Those left, ask

       and wait;

             are given
hope and reason to hope and reason
to have reason to hope, when we know
their lost ones are ash from a fire,
blown across the borders, blown into
the controlled zones, the holding pens,

the hangars and arrival halls of hell.

Found Near the Body of Humfrey Coningsby

Possessions: clothing; stained, repaired,
well-worn and of the English style
(which is both affected and badly
stitched). Leg-wear: short boots, worn
on all sides, as if the owner kicked
continuously. A pack: to be carried
by a horse. No horse to speak of.
Weapons: long sword, short knife,
sharp sticks but blunt; dice,
assorted bones. Other items: books,
two; paper, small sheets; cards and
pieces of glass; a cloak of gold,
a white hourglass of seahorse tooth;
a map of an unknown region; a bible
spewed out in a foreign tongue – could
be Welsh, probably not – un-annotated,
slightly singed, smelling of new sweat.

Inscription made in 1624, All Saints Church, Neen Sollars

Man stay, see, read, muse, mourn and mind thy end.
Flesh, pomp, time, thoughts, world, wealth as wind doeth pass.
Love, fear, hate, hope, fast, pray, feed, give amend.
Man, beast, fish, fowl and all flesh else is grass.
See, hear thyself frailties as in a glass.
No odds between us but uncertain hours
Which are prescribed by the Heavenly Powers,
For Death, in fine, all kind of flesh be ours.

Respice Finem

Farewell then Sister Flesh and think of me.

Textual Notes

The June drop – excess or sub-standard fruit shed naturally by apple trees in early summer.

Leather-coats – apples, of russet appearance with very hard skins.

Mahomet (or Mehmet) the Third (1566 – 1603), Crown Prince, later Sultan, of the Ottoman Empire, Caliph of Islam.

The Siege of Strigonium – also known as the Siege of Gran, in Hungary, led by Christian forces against the Ottomans in September, 1595.

Corley Rocks – an outcrop of sandstone near the village of Corley, north-west of Coventry, England.

B17 – the flagship model from bicycle saddle makers, Brooks of Smethwick, England.

Prince Rudolf – Rudolf II (1552 – 1612), Holy Roman Emperor, King of Hungary and Croatia, King of Bohemia and Archduke of Austria.

Respice Finem – 'look to the end'.